THIS BOOK IS NO LONGER THE PROPERTY OF
THE UNIVERSITY OF CHICAGO LIBRARY

Predicting the Unpredictable?

Science and Guesswork in
Financial Market Forecasting

TERENCE C. MILLS

*Professor of Applied Economics,
University of Hull*

Institute of Economic Affairs
1992

First published in October 1992
by
THE INSTITUTE OF ECONOMIC AFFAIRS
2 Lord North Street, Westminster, London SW1P 3LB

© The Institute of Economic Affairs 1992

Occasional Paper 87

All rights reserved

ISSN 0073-909X

ISBN 0-255 36310-9

The Institute gratefully acknowledges financial support for its publications programme and other work from a generous benefaction by the late Alec and Beryl Warren.

All the Institute's publications seek to further its objective of promoting the advancement of learning, by research into economic and political science, by education of the public therein, and by the dissemination of ideas, research and the results of research in these subjects. The views expressed are those of the author, not of the IEA, which has no corporate view.

Printed in Great Britain by
GORON PRO-PRINT CO LTD, LANCING, WEST SUSSEX
Set in Berthold Plantin 11 on 13 point

Contents

FOREWORD	*Colin Robinson*	5
THE AUTHOR		9
1. Introduction		11
2. The Origin of 'Technical Analysis'		11
The Art of 'Chartism'		12
3. The Statistical Analysis of Financial Data		14
4. Random Walks – Into Error?		16
Efficient Markets Hypothesis		20
5. The Efficient Markets Hypothesis: Three Versions		22
6. The Evidence For and Against the EMH		23
Stock Market Anomalies		24
Usefulness of Non-Linear Models		26
7. Long-term Predictability in Stock Markets		27
Long-Horizon Returns in the UK		29
8. Other Financial Markets		30
Research on the London Foreign Exchange Market		31
9. Are Markets Interlinked?		32
Interactions Between Stock and Gilt Markets		33
10. Conclusions		36

FIGURES:

1.	'Head and Shoulders'	13
2.	FT – Actuaries 500 Index: Index and Simulated Index, 1980-90	15
3.	FT – Actuaries 500 Index: Price Changes, 1980-90	17
4.	FT – Actuaries 500 Index: Actual Path and Chartist Prediction, 1984-86	18
5a.	Price and Dividend Indices, 1969-88	34
5b.	Stock Prices and Gilt Yields, 1969-88	34
6.	'Confidence', 1969-88	35

GLOSSARY 37

BIBLIOGRAPHY 43

SUMMARY .. .. *Back cover*

Foreword

HUMAN DESIRE for knowledge of the future is so deep-seated that, from the earliest times, people have sought means of making predictions. Dreams were once believed to foreshadow future events. In the forty-first chapter of Genesis, for example, Pharaoh asked Joseph to interpret his two dreams in which seven fat cattle were devoured by seven thin cattle and seven good ears of corn were consumed by seven poor ears. Joseph, with the aid of a divine revelation, produced a perfect forecast — that seven years of prosperity would be succeeded by seven years of famine. One of the few recorded examples of successful central planning followed: the people of Egypt were fed because (since the future was known) excess stocks of corn could be placed in store for seven years and then extracted for use during the years of poor harvests.

An alternative to dream-interpretation is consultation of oracles. Investigations by social anthropologists of societies we regard as 'primitive' show extensive use of oracles and magic to make predictions. Simple oracles are consulted both for everyday decisions – for instance, whether to undertake a journey today or tomorrow – or for more momentous matters – such as whether to undertake marriage to a given person.

The innate desire for knowledge of the future stems from two features of life which are central to economic thought – the need to choose among alternatives and the uncertainty of the future. Because, as Lionel Robbins pointed out, resources are limited whereas wants are essentially unlimited, life is a series of choices in which each decision to do something necessarily implies a decision not to do something else; therefore the real cost of each decision is the opportunity forgone (or 'opportunity cost'). Moreover, since the consequences of life's decisions all lie in an uncertain future, those decisions are always taken in states of semi-ignorance: we can only make informed guesses about the consequences of our actions and our forecasts will frequently turn out to be wildly inaccurate. Nevertheless, we have no choice but to attempt predictions, since they are implicit in every decision.

The paradox that forecasting is inevitable but (in the strict sense) impossible is resolved in a competitive market economy by competition in forecasting. Each individual and each organisation makes its own forecasts, explicit or implicit, as a basis for decisions. Even though none of the forecasts will be precisely correct (except by chance), some will be better than others. Other things equal, better forecasters will make better decisions and so there is a process of forecaster selection. The centrally planned economy tries to eliminate competition in forecasting, as in other things, by forcing everyone to act on the basis of the same set of (incorrect) forecasts: that is one of the main reasons why central plans collapse.

Oracles, magicians and dream-interpreters have been replaced by modellers who attempt, principally by analysis of past experience, to make systematic use of history to peer into the future. The modellers are not always more successful. In Britain, macro-economic forecasting has fallen into disrepute after recent well-publicised failures. In individual markets, however, where qualitative market knowledge can be used in combination with quantitative models, forecasters appear to have been more successful.

But perhaps such apparent success is just an illusion. Perhaps there are fundamental reasons why any attempt at forecasting is doomed to failure. In *Occasional Paper No. 87*, Professor Terence Mills examines that issue with reference to financial markets – which, with large numbers of participants and rapid information flows, come closest to the 'perfect' markets of elementary economic theory. Information from forecasts will always feed back into decisions – indeed that is their purpose. Consequently, it is possible that forecasts will always either be self-fulfilling or self-defeating because they affect the future. A forecast that a currency would be devalued might well be self-fulfilling if enough people believed it. Joseph's forecast, on the other hand, was self-defeating because action was taken to avoid the events foreseen. Testing the accuracy of a forecast, *ex post*, is therefore always difficult because the forecast may have been one of the principal determinants of the future.

Even worse for the forecaster, as Mills points out, if markets are 'efficient' – broadly, that they instantly incorporate all relevant available information – market prices must incorporate forecasts. If the stock market is efficient, for instance, as soon as a forecast about a given stock is made, it will immediately be reflected in the price. Feedback is therefore instantaneous as the anticipated future becomes the present. In such circumstances, forecasts will not allow those producing them to make 'excess profits' because any forecasts known to the market are immediately incorporated in the relevant price.

In examining whether or not there are 'anomalies' in market prices which could be exploited by skilled forecasters, Mills considers the post-war history of attempts to forecast financial markets, starting from the efforts of Arthur Ellinger and other 'chartists' in the 1950s. Chartism, which still has its advocates, assumes that charts of past behaviour contain information patterns (such as the 'head-and-shoulders') which are of value in predicting future behaviour. On this view, studying a time-series of past price movements can yield useful information about what will happen without the need for complex models which attempt to find explanations for movements in the price of a particular stock or in a market index.

Mills then examines statistical techniques which go beyond 'eyeballing'. He shows, using simple examples, why academic researchers have claimed that stock market prices will follow a 'random walk' and are essentially unpredictable. If financial markets are efficient, they will immediately incorporate any new information (including forecasts) which reaches them. Therefore 'new' information arriving in an efficient market must, by definition, always be unpredictable – otherwise it would already have been incorporated in prices. Yet prices which change only in response to hitherto unpredictable information must move unpredictably! As Professor Mills says,

> 'Randomly evolving prices are ... the necessary consequence of intelligent investors competing to discover relevant information on

which to buy or sell stocks *before* the rest of the market becomes aware of that information. Indeed, if stock price movements were predictable, that would constitute evidence of stock market inefficiency . . .' (p. 20).

Despite the theoretical attractions of the unpredictability thesis and much statistical evidence which, for many years, appeared to favour it, Mills explains that researchers have recently discovered various 'anomalies' which suggest a degree of predictability. For example, in some markets there appear to be 'calendar effects' – which indicate that prices move in particular directions at particular times of the day, week, month or year – although it is puzzling why traders do not exploit them. Other research suggests that, both in the United States and Britain, long-term returns on equities may to some extent be predictable from past data. In the bond and foreign exchange markets, there is again evidence that prices may not follow random walks.

Professor Mills is careful to explain that his purpose is not to pour scorn on chartists and others who use relatively simple methods to analyse financial markets. He concludes that the anomalies revealed by recent detailed research suggest that

> 'financial markets are often predictable to some extent, but the crucial question is whether this predictability can be exploited to make excess profits from trading in the markets. It is probably very difficult to do so, but that is unlikely to deter analysts and researchers from continuing to try to detect anomalies in the hope of uncovering, if only for a short while, a trading strategy that will "beat the market"' (p. 36).

In this *Occasional Paper*, Terence Mills reviews and makes accessible to the non-specialist a body of post-war research on financial markets which has wide-ranging practical and theoretical implications. Although the views expressed in the *Paper* are those of the author and not those of the Institute (which has no corporate view), its Trustees, its Directors or its Advisers, the IEA offers Professor Mills's *Paper* as a succinct and readable discussion of issues of interest not only to practitioners in financial markets but to anyone interested in finance.

October 1992 COLIN ROBINSON
Editorial Director, Institute of Economic Affairs,
and University of Surrey

The Author

TERENCE C. MILLS is currently Professor of Applied Economics and Dean of the School of Economic Studies at the University of Hull. He is a graduate of the universities of Essex and Warwick, where his PhD thesis investigated the econometric relationships between money, output, prices and interest rates in the UK. From 1976 to 1988 he was Lecturer in Econometrics at the University of Leeds, and between 1980 and 1984 he was also attached to the Monetary Policy Group at the Bank of England. Between 1988 and 1990 he was successively Senior, then Professorial, Research Fellow at the Centre for Financial Markets, City University Business School.

He is author of *Time Series Techniques for Economists*, published in 1990 by Cambridge University Press, who are also publishing his latest book, *The Econometric Modelling of Financial Time Series*, in 1993. He is the author of some 60 articles in journals and edited books, primarily on applying time-series techniques to issues in macro-economics, monetary economics, economic history and financial markets.

Predicting the Unpredictable?
TERENCE C. MILLS

1. Introduction

THE PREDICTABILITY of financial markets has engaged the attention of market professionals and academic economists and statisticians for many years and has also attracted the interest of numerous 'amateur' investors, whether gifted or otherwise. Perhaps unusually for economics, the subject of financial market predictability also offers an illuminating example of how 'real world' market experience and 'ivory tower' academic theories have evolved and influenced each other as more and more research, not only in universities but also in financial institutions such as stockbrokers and banks, has been undertaken. The most recent upsurge in interest has come about through quantitative economists utilising the benefits conferred by the rapid development of high-speed and easily accessible computers using sophisticated statistical software.

2. The Origin of 'Technical Analysis'

DETAILED ANALYSIS of the financial markets in the UK began in the early 1950s; the Society of Investment Analysts was founded soon afterwards. One of the earliest investment analysts to focus on the study of past price movements and patterns was Arthur Ellinger, whose book, *The Art of Investment*, originally published in 1955, became the first UK text on a subject that now goes under the name of *'technical analysis'** or, to use a term more redolent of the techniques used, *'chartism'**.[1]

Ellinger's mode of analysis was to use charts of past prices to

---

*Words and phrases set in italics and followed by an asterisk are defined/explained in the 'Glossary', below, pp. 37-41.

[1] Ellinger (1971).

predict future movements in the price, for example, of a share quoted on the stock exchange. He remarks:

> 'It is probably true that the majority of investors believe that a price chart, whether it records the movement of a share or that of a market average, is nothing more than a historical record. They say, "That's the past; what I want to know is the future." They are probably unwise in despising the past from which it is usually possible to draw useful lessons, but the point on which we disagree most strongly is that the chart is only a historical record. It deals not only with the past but with the present; in addition to providing a historical record it offers a current commentary as well.'[1]

Ellinger thought of a financial market as always looking for the 'right' price. Although he did not define that price explicitly, there was no suggestion that it would be a constant, for he saw price movements as falling into three classes. The primary trend was the main direction in which the market carried out its search for the right price: these trend movements usually lasted for more than a year and sometimes for much longer periods. Secondary trends zig-zagged up and down across the axis of the primary trend; these were the directions in which the market sought the right price for periods of at least several weeks and perhaps many months. Finally, tertiary trends wandered across the axis of the secondary trends; they endured for a day or two and at most for a few weeks.

The Art of 'Chartism'

For Ellinger, who advocated long-term investment, the main purpose of reading charts was to decide on the direction of the primary trend and to determine, as early as possible, if it had changed: as he remarked, trends go on until they stop! Speculators and short-term investors, on the other hand, attempt to determine whether tertiary or secondary trends have changed. The 'art' of chartism is to identify trend changes by assessing whether certain price patterns, regarded by chartists as having prophetic significance, in the sense that they are believed regularly to precede trend changes, have occurred or, indeed, are occurring.

[1] Ellinger (1971, p. 121).

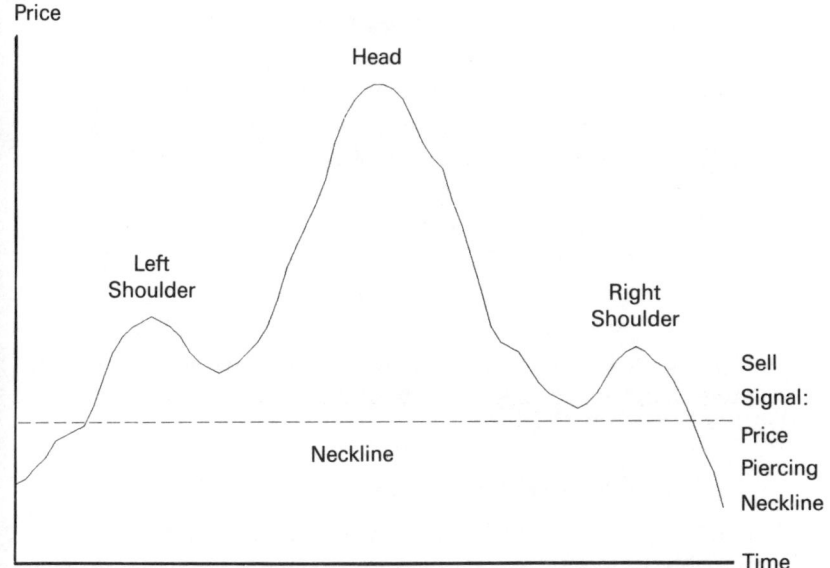

Figure 1
'Head and Shoulders'

There are many chartist patterns, of varying degrees of complexity, going by such evocative terms as 'gaps', 'flags', 'pennants', 'symmetrical triangles', 'rising wedges', 'resistance lines', 'reflecting barriers', and such like.[1] Perhaps the most celebrated of the *reversal* patterns, in that it is frequently referred to in the press, is the 'head-and-shoulders'. This signals a move in the primary trend from upswing to downswing (or *vice versa*) and is illustrated in Figure 1. The left shoulder is formed by a price rise and then a decline. The head is then formed by a rise to a higher point than the preceding rise and a decline to about the same price level that existed at the beginning of the head formation. The right shoulder is formed by a rise that fails to penetrate the high price of the head and declines to a lower point than any of the other prices in the formation. A 'neckline' can then be drawn through the pattern: when the falling price penetrates the neckline through the right shoulder, this constitutes a signal to sell, as the price trend has now turned

[1] Stewart (1986) provides an extended discussion of these and others.

ineluctably into a downward (or bear) movement. Stewart maintains that 'the "forecast" from a head and shoulders is for a fall equal in extent to the distance from the top of the head (the peak) to the neckline'.[1]

Technical analysis has, in recent years, evolved further in the sense that attempts have been made to provide a theoretical underpinning to what, on the face of it, is a purely descriptive forecasting technique. Plummer, for example, invokes the psychology of crowd behaviour and the mathematics of spirals, notably limit cycles and Fibonacci Sequences, to provide what he regards as a formal underpinning to technical analysis, concluding that '[i]nvestors who follow the rules ... should, after a little experience, find it entirely possible to embark on a long-term programme of accumulating wealth'.[2]

3. The Statistical Analysis of Financial Data

EVEN WHILE this 'eyeball' examination of past price patterns for possible prophetic significance was becoming a standard technique for some investment analysts, academics had begun to analyse financial price series using statistical techniques and 'calculating machines', rather than simply graph paper. As early as 1953, the distinguished British statistician, Sir Maurice Kendall, found that *changes* in security prices behaved nearly as if they had been generated by a suitably designed roulette wheel for which each outcome was statistically independent of past outcomes and for which probabilities of occurrence were reasonably stable through time.[3] The implication is that, once an investor accumulates enough evidence to make good estimates of the probabilities of different outcomes of the wheel, his predictions can be based only on those probabilities, and need pay no attention to the pattern of recent spins. Such spins are relevant to prediction only insofar as they contribute to more precise estimates of probabilities. In gambling terms, Kendall's roulette wheel 'has no memory'.

Similar conclusions had, in fact, been reached long before

[1] Stewart (1986, p. 16). [3] Kendall (1953).
[2] Plummer (1989, p. 229).

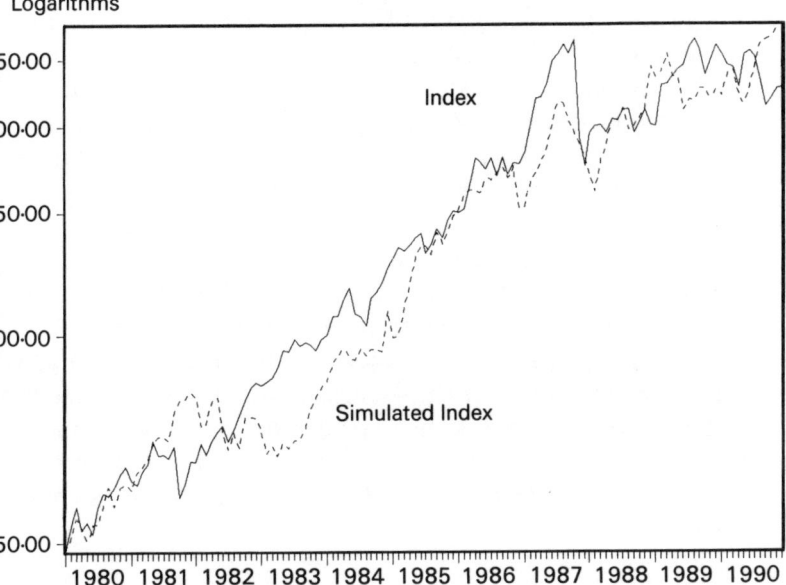

Figure 2
FT – Actuaries 500 Index, 1980-90

Kendall's study, most notably by Holbrook Working in 1934, but had not been widely disseminated.[1] Harry Roberts gave further impetus to this line of argument by presenting an example which was to have a major influence on the way most academics think about how financial markets 'work'.[2] Roberts's example was based on constructing an artificial series using the 'chance' model discussed above and comparing it with an observed stock price series: his argument can be illustrated with an example drawn from recent UK stock market experience.

Figure 2 shows end-month observations on the logarithm of the *Financial Times – Actuaries 500* UK stock market index for the period from January 1980 to December 1990. The pattern is familiar to those who follow long-term movements in the stock market – a fairly steady upward movement (primarily a consequence of the underlying increase in the general price level), about which there are many short-term fluctuations, most

[1] Working (1934).   [2] Roberts (1959).

[15]

notably the rapid increase in share prices after the 'Big Bang' of 1986 culminating in the 'Crash' of October 1987.

A good fit to these observed UK stock market movements can be obtained by a Kendall or Roberts type of model in which stock prices move randomly about a long-term upward trend.[1] A simulation of this type of model gives the series superimposed on Figure 2. Although the two series are not identical, their general features are very similar, even to the extent that the simulated series gives a fair impression of a big bang boom in 1986 and subsequent crash in 1987.

This model states that the change in the (logarithms of the) series is, on average, positive, thus giving the upward drift of the price level, but that these changes are completely random and hence unpredictable: it is thus equivalent to the Kendall chance model. Indeed, formal statistical analysis of the price index shows that such a model can be regarded as essentially reproducing the behaviour of the index in all its essential details.

4. Random Walks – Into Error?

THIS MODEL is known as a *random walk with drift**. The term 'random walk' often intrigues people not familiar with the jargon of time-series analysis. It is believed that the term was first used in an exchange of correspondence appearing in *Nature* in 1905 between Karl Pearson and Lord Rayleigh, which provided the answer to the following problem: If one leaves a drunk in an empty field in the dead of night and wishes to find him some time later while it is still dark, what is the optimal search strategy? It is to start exactly where the drunk had been placed and to walk in a straight line away from that point in any direction you wish. The reasoning behind this strategy is that

[1] A more formal statement of the model is:
log price at month t = previous month's log price (i.e. at month $t-1$) + ·0115 + random term,
where ·0115 is the inflationary 'drift' of the series and the random term is a drawing from a normal distribution with zero mean and a standard deviation of ·0564, and where the series begins (at month 0, corresponding to January 1980) at a value of 5·5 (these values were set equal to the drift and standard deviation of the actual (logarithmic) price index).

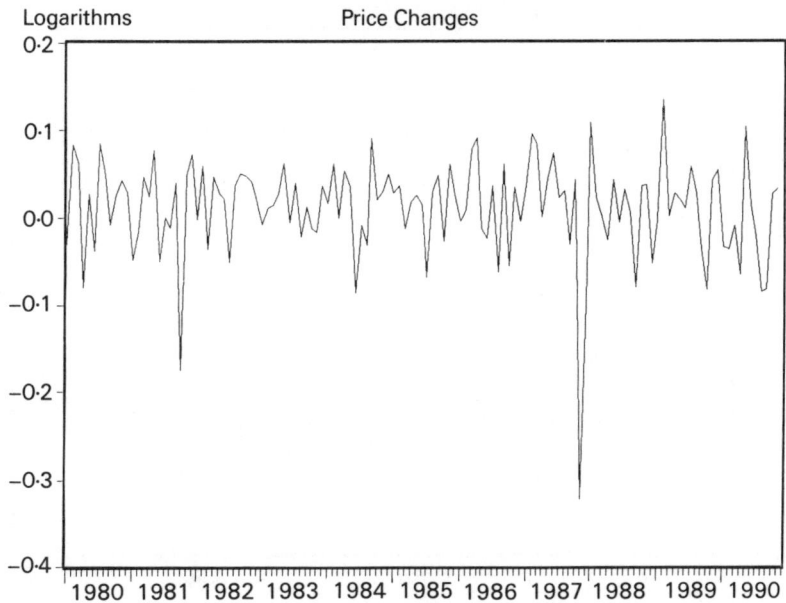

Figure 3
FT – Actuaries 500 Index, 1980-90

this point is an unbiased estimate of the drunk's future position since he will presumably stagger along in an unpredictable and random fashion.

This example illustrates the crucial property of a random walk. In the present context, if prices follow a random walk, then the optimal forecast of *any* future price, made using the information contained in past prices, is simply today's price (perhaps adjusted by the drift): analysing the past history of prices is doomed to failure. Any patterns observed in the past occurred by chance, and will thus have zero probability of ever occurring again.

Why should people be fooled into seeing patterns in series that are no more than accumulations of random numbers? After all, the changes in the price index, shown in Figure 3, look completely independent and, indeed, formal statistical tests cannot reject such a hypothesis. This self-deception seems to be because there is a tendency to ascribe to *sums* of independent

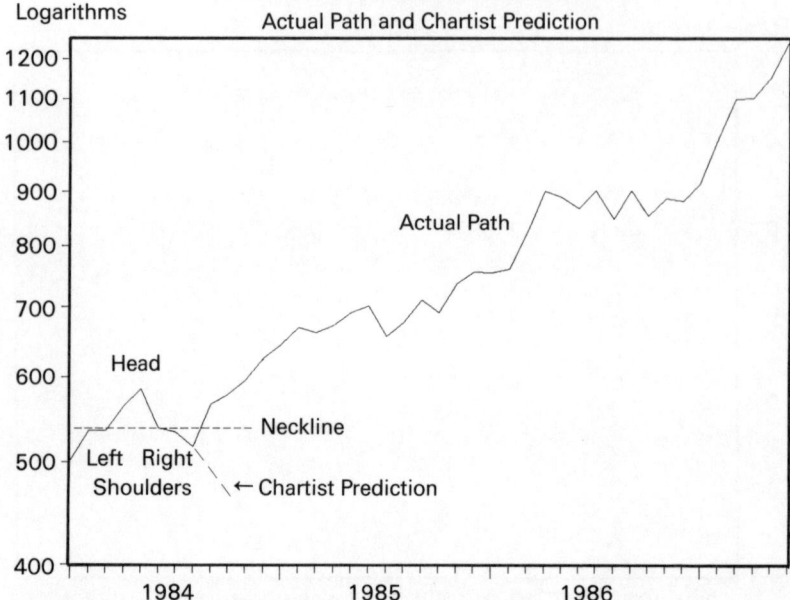

*random variables** behaviour which is typical of the individual random variables themselves. Hence, if price changes are indeed random, the price level, which is the sum of the changes, will be expected to be random as well, although it will, in fact, be highly correlated with past price levels. Conversely, when patterns are observed in the levels, price changes will be expected to be related.[1]

An entertaining example of people being fooled in this way is the behaviour of the UK stock price index during the early part of 1984. Figure 4 shows the price index for the first six months of that year. To chartists at the time, this revealed an unmistakable 'head-and-shoulders' pattern (the pattern is even clearer from daily observations of the index, which is what chartists typically examine). The unanimity of chartists led to an article being

---

[1] This counter-intuitive result is, in fact, a consequence of the *first arc sine law* of probability and is typical of many problems involving the cumulation of chance fluctuations: Feller (1959, Chapter 3) provides the classic discussion of the underlying probability theory and its applications.

published in the *Observer* on 15 July 1984, entitled prophetically 'Sign of the bear forms in the charts', in which various chartists gave their views of future trends in the financial markets. Two of the numerous quotes are worth reporting, although names will not be mentioned so as to protect the gullible! The first is:

> 'The bull market is over. There is no doubting the chart pattern called the "head-and-shoulders". The pattern cannot be ignored because experience shows that it is possibly the strongest and most reliable pattern share prices can make.'

The second remarks that

> 'the "head-and-shoulders" are clear enough, even if the head is a bit lopsided and the right shoulder is hunched'.

All were agreed that the stock market would drop considerably, a rough consensus being that the fall would be around 35 per cent of the level at the 'head'. Instead, the very next month the index turned up again and proceeded to rise consistently for the next three years before the Crash of October 1987: the overall upward movement, which began in 1975, was the longest bull market on record!

Why should stock market prices follow random walks? Suppose that the price of a stock, say Marks & Spencer, was predictable, that the model for making these predictions was known to investors, and that it was predicting that the price, currently 300 pence, would rise in three days to 330 pence. What would investors do? Obviously, they would place a large wave of immediate buy orders to cash in on the prospective increase in price. No one holding Marks & Spencer shares, however, would be willing to sell. The net effect would be an *immediate* jump in the price to 330p. The forecast of a future price increase would thus lead to an immediate price increase, reflecting the 'good news' implicit in the prediction.

More generally, we might argue that *any* information which is accessible to investors and which could be used to predict stock performance must *already* be reflected in stock prices, otherwise any 'news' indicating that the stock is underpriced, for example, so that a profit opportunity is offered, would lead to investors flocking to buy the stock and immediately bidding up its price, the rise only ending when the stock is no longer regarded as underpriced, that is, when the price has reached a 'fair' level.

However, if prices are bid immediately to such 'fair' levels, it must be that they can move only in response to *new* information. This new information must be unpredictable; if it could be predicted, the prediction would already be part of today's information. Thus prices that change in response to new, and hence unpredictable, information must also move unpredictably.

Efficient Markets Hypothesis

This is the essence of the argument that changes in stock prices will be random and unpredictable – that prices will follow a random walk. Randomly evolving prices are, therefore, the necessary consequence of intelligent investors competing to discover relevant information on which to buy or sell stocks *before* the rest of the market becomes aware of that information. Indeed, if stock price movements were predictable, that would constitute evidence of stock market inefficiency, because the ability to predict prices would indicate that all available information was not already reflected in stock prices: the notion that prices already reflect all available information is referred to as the *efficient markets hypothesis**, often shortened to the EMH.[1]

Formal mathematical proofs of the EMH were developed by Paul Samuelson and Benoit Mandlebrot but, surprisingly, much of this work had been anticipated in 1900 by the French mathematician Louis Bachelier in a remarkable PhD thesis in which he developed an elaborate mathematical theory of speculative prices, which he then tested on the pricing of French government bonds, finding that such prices were consistent with the random walk model.[2] Even more remarkable, Bachelier's thesis also developed many of the mathematical properties of Brownian motion which had been thought to have first been derived some years later in the physical sciences, particularly by

---

[1] Most of the early papers examining the random walk model are contained in the collection of Cootner (1964), while Granger and Morgenstern (1970) provide a detailed development and empirical examination of the model and various of its refinements.

[2] See Samuelson (1965), Mandelbrot (1966) and Bachelier (1900, English translation in Cootner, 1964).

Einstein! Yet, as Mandelbrot remarks, Bachelier had great difficulty in even finding himself a university appointment, let alone disseminating his theories throughout the academic community![1]

Strictly, the term random walk refers to a sequence of price changes that are independent of each other. While this is a useful way of *empirically* representing stock prices, it has led to some serious questions being raised about the validity of the random walk hypothesis as a *theoretical* model of financial markets. The work of Samuelson and Mandelbrot emphasised that the assumption of price change independence is too restrictive to enable the random walk model to be derived from any reasonable optimising model of financial market behaviour.

A model that is appropriate, however, is one in which expected *returns* are constant, and where the returns sequence is uncorrelated. (The return on a stock is equivalent to the logarithmic change in the price, including dividend payments. Since these dividend payments accrue only at certain times and are usually small relative to the price, the return, for our expository purpose, may be taken to be the same as the logarithmic price change itself. This will not be the case, for example, in applications using stock market indices observed at monthly or longer intervals.) The model implies that prices (strictly prices plus reinvested dividends) follow a *martingale** process and this distinction, as we shall see, can be important in more detailed investigations into market efficiency.[2]

Why should stock prices be expected to reflect 'all available information'? After all, if you are willing to spend time and money on gathering information, it might seem reasonable that you could turn up something overlooked by the rest of the investment community. It is precisely because information may

---

[1] Mandelbrot (1989).

[2] A martingale is the mathematical formulation of a 'fair game'. The term, which also denotes part of a horse's harness or a ship's rigging, refers in addition to a gambling system, originally popular with the inhabitants of the village of Martigues in France, in which the stake is doubled after each losing bet: a usage that may be felt to be rather apposite when considering the behaviour of financial data! An excellent, though technically demanding, survey of these issues is provided by LeRoy (1989).

be costly to uncover and analyse that investors will have an incentive to spend such time and resources on analysing and uncovering new information only if such activity is likely to generate higher investment returns.

Given the size of today's pension and unit trust funds, small relative increases in investment performance can produce large financial rewards, so many fund managers are willing to spend large sums on industry analysts, computer support, and research effort. With so many well-backed, highly paid and aggressive analysts willing to spend considerable resources on research, there will not be many easy pickings in the market. Competition among them ensures that, as a general rule, prices ought to reflect available information regarding their proper, 'fair' levels.

5. The Efficient Markets Hypothesis: Three Versions

IT IS COMMON to distinguish between three versions of the EMH: the weak, semi-strong, and strong forms, which differ by their notions of what is meant by the term 'all available information'.

The *weak* form of the hypothesis corresponds to the situation considered so far: it asserts that the current price already reflects all the information that can be derived from examining the history of past prices. Such histories are readily available and virtually costless to obtain: for example, they can be obtained from organisations such as *Datastream*. Weak form efficiency holds that if such data ever conveyed reliable signals about future performance, all investors would have learned already to exploit them, so that buy signals, for example, would result in an immediate price increase. This idea is diametrically opposed to the beliefs of chartists, whose views imply a sluggish response by prices to changes in the underlying 'fundamentals' so that any changes in trend can be identified by the price tracing out one of the prophetic patterns.

The *semi-strong* form of the hypothesis goes further and states that all *publicly available* information on the prospects of a firm must already be reflected in the price. Such information includes, in addition to past prices, fundamental data on the firm's product line, quality of management, balance sheet composition, earnings forecasts, and so on. Again, if investors had access to such information from publicly available sources, one would expect it to be reflected in the price.

Finally, the *strong* form of the EMH states that prices reflect *all* information relevant to the firm, even information available only to company insiders. This is, therefore, an extreme version of the hypothesis, for it implies that individuals who have access to pertinent information before it comes into the public domain still cannot profit from trading on it: there are thus no abnormal returns to be made from insider dealing!

The semi-strong form of the EMH has important implications for attempts to predict the behaviour of a market index (rather than a single price). It implies that past movements in other indices related to the market – such as dividends and earnings, past movements in the indices of other markets (say, the gilts and exchange markets or other international stock markets), and even past movements in economic variables (for example, the money supply and industrial output) – have no predictive ability.

6. The Evidence For and Against the EMH

THE EMH thus presents a clear hypothesis which can be tested with easily obtainable, accurate data – a situation that is rather unusual in economics. It is little wonder, then, that the EMH has become one of the most tested propositions in economics, with findings that throw up many intriguing insights into the workings of modern day financial markets. Given the profusion of such tests, which use many countries, data bases and observation periods, it is best to concentrate on those findings which seem to offer evidence that might lead to a better understanding of the behaviour of financial markets.

The first tests of the EMH or, to be more precise, of whether stock prices are really unpredictable, were presented by Eugene Fama in a classic 1965 paper, which begins:

'For many years the following question has been a source of continuing controversy in both academic and business circles: To what extent can the past history of a common stock's price be used to make meaningful predictions concerning the future price of the stock?'[1]

[1] Fama (1965).

He concludes some 60 pages later: 'It seems safe to say that this paper has presented strong and voluminous evidence in favour of the random walk hypothesis.' Yet, over 20 years later, a paper by Fama and Kenneth French has a rather different opening sentence: 'There is much evidence that stock returns are predictable.'[1]

What made Fama change his views? For many years after 1965, nothing did. Few studies were able to reject the random walk hypothesis. Those that did could not demonstrate that, once trading costs were taken into account, the use of a trading rule utilising the observed predictability of returns could perform better than the simple buy-and-hold strategy that is an implication of the EMH.

As advanced computing power facilitated the establishment of larger data banks and the development of more complex statistical models, so the alternative hypotheses to the random walk became more refined. As anyone engaged in hypothesis testing in any discipline quickly realises, the powers of statistical tests are substantially increased when alternatives to a null hypothesis (that is, a hypothesis implied by a specific theory) are obtained themselves by specific, rather than general, theories. By the early 1980s evidence had begun to accumulate of a number of rejections of the random walk hypothesis in favour of specific, and often peculiar, alternatives.

Stock Market Anomalies

Many of these 'anomalies', as they are referred to in the finance literature, appear to be 'calendar effects'. Evidence from the United States, reported in Thaler (1987a, 1987b), has established the presence of the following anomalies:

○ a 'January effect', during which month prices tend to rise far more than the average monthly amount, particularly the prices of small firms and firms whose price had declined substantially over the past few years;

○ a 'weekend effect', in which the typical three-day Friday-to-

[1] Fama and French (1988).

Monday return is negative, rather than the hypothesised three times the typical weekday return;

o a 'holiday effect', in which returns on days immediately preceding a holiday were *fourteen* times higher than the typical daily return;

o a 'turn of the month' effect, which was isolated by examining daily returns on the Dow Jones index for a period of 90 years, and shows that, aside from four days around the turn of the month when returns are extremely large, the index generally falls;

o and various 'intra-day' effects, which were isolated by examining a time-ordered record of every stock transaction (all 15 million!) made on the New York Stock Exchange for the 14 months between December 1981 and February 1983. The weekend effect, for example, spills over into the first 45 minutes of trading on Monday, with prices falling during this period. On all other days, prices rise significantly during the first 45 minutes, while returns are high near the very end of the day, particularly on the last trade of the day.

While these effects are not large enough for traders with significant transactions costs to exploit, they nevertheless remain a genuine puzzle, for those investors who plan to trade anyway could alter the timing of their trading to take advantage of the predictable price changes. A number of explanations have been offered, all based on 'institutional' considerations, such as the timing of flows of funds into and out of the market, and the practice of investment managers to 'window dress', that is, to clean up their portfolios by getting rid of embarrassing holdings before reporting dates, which tend to coincide with natural calendar dates such as year-ends and month-ends.

These anomalies have all been isolated by analysing considerable amounts of high frequency data to find significant correlations between price changes at various points of the calendar. Such large data sets can also be used to test more formal alternatives to the random walk hypothesis. Standard statistical tests of the random walk hypothesis actually test whether price changes (or, equivalently, returns) are uncorrelated over time, rather than independent. As any tyro statistician soon finds, whereas the assumption of *independence** implies the absence of *correlation**, the converse, that the absence of correlation implies independence, does not necessarily hold. If we restrict ourselves to analysing only *linear models**, that is, those in which only linear combinations of past price changes are considered, this distinction is immaterial, but if we consider non-linear alternatives to the random walk, it becomes very important indeed.

Usefulness of Non-Linear Models

Non-linear models* allow more general combinations of past price changes to be considered, such as products and, in particular, functions of previous forecast errors, which allow the *volatility** of prices to be incorporated as an explanatory factor. With such models it is possible for price changes to be uncorrelated but not independent, so that future price changes may be somewhat predictable. Indeed, in many of the non-linear models currently being investigated, predictability comes not through being able to forecast the price changes themselves, but being able to forecast the *variance* of the changes, so that although the best *point* forecast of a price change may be, say, zero, the width of forecast *intervals* will depend on how volatile the series has been in the recent past.

Such models, which are consistent with the martingale assumption of efficient markets (which only rules out any predictability of price changes), are now a major research topic in the analysis of financial markets since they can model formally the well-documented observation that financial series go through protracted periods of tranquillity interspersed by bursts of turbulence, in which large price changes are often followed by large changes in the opposite direction. The type of models that seem to fit the data best are either of the 'bilinear' class or the class going under the almost incomprehensible, at least to non-time series analysts, title of *autoregressive conditionally heteroskedastic**, known by the acronym of ARCH; indeed, the *Journal of Econometrics* has devoted an entire issue to the application of such models to finance.[1]

[1] *Journal of Econometrics*, Vol. 52, No. 1/2, 1992.

Detecting departures from linearity, which was previously very difficult, has now become feasible by using large data sets and harnessing considerable computing power. Such detection has become increasingly important given the upsurge in interest in *chaotic dynamics**: models which generate observations that look completely unpredictable when subjected to standard statistical tests but which are *perfectly* predictable when the generating mechanism is known. The interest in such models is hardly surprising. If seemingly unpredictable price changes were generated by a chaotic process, the discovery of which would enable them to be predicted without error, there would be huge potential for profitable trading.

Such potential does not, however, appear to exist: while researchers are beginning to uncover much evidence of non-linearity in financial data, such departures from linearity seem to be almost certainly stochastic (that is, not perfectly predictable).[1] Neftci shows that only if a financial time-series is non-linear can such techniques be useful, but if it is, certain chartist rules may capture some information ignored by formal linear prediction theory.[2]

7. Long-term Predictability in Stock Markets

ALTHOUGH THIS PAPER has concentrated so far on detecting departures from unpredictability in data observed at very high frequencies, there is also considerable interest in the predictability of returns calculated over much longer time-horizons of up to 10 years or more. The stimulus for this research was provided by theoretical models focussing on the idea that fashions, or 'fads', in investor attitudes may affect stock prices.[3]

These theories consider markets containing both rational 'information' traders and irrational 'liquidity' or 'noise' traders, sometimes referred to in the literature as 'blockheads'; the presence of the latter introduces inefficiencies into the market

---

[1] See, for example, the detailed results reported by Hsieh (1991) and Ramsey (1990).

[2] Neftci (1991).

[3] These theories are surveyed by Robert Shiller, one of the major proponents of fads models, in his collection of essays, *Market Volatility* (1989).

which are characterised by prices taking long, but temporary, swings away from their 'fair', or 'fundamental', values. Such swings induce negative autocorrelation into sequences of returns (that is, a tendency for high returns to be followed by low returns). Although weak for the short horizons, daily or weekly, commonly analysed in traditional tests of market efficiency, this autocorrelation can nevertheless be quite large in long-horizon returns. Such negative autocorrelation is often referred to as *mean reversion**, since returns must have this property if divergences between market and fundamental values are to be eliminated.

When studied from this perspective, long-horizon returns on United States equities do appear to be somewhat predictable: between 25 and 40 per cent of the variation in five-year returns is explainable by past returns; moreover, the relationship between current and past long-horizon returns is significantly negative, thus supporting the presence of mean reversion.

There is also evidence for a second type of mean reversion, in which a 'contrarian' strategy of purchasing stocks whose prices seem low relative to their fundamental values is found to yield better than average returns. De Bondt and Thaler review research that shows that a strategy of buying stocks with low price to earnings per share (P/E) ratios yields 'abnormal' returns over and above the 'normal' returns required for adequate risk compensation.[1] An explanation for this is that companies with low P/Es are temporarily undervalued because the market becomes inappropriately pessimistic about current and future earnings. Eventually, however, actual earnings growth differs predictably from forecast earnings growth, in due course leading to price corrections and hence to the P/E anomaly. Similar results have been found for other contrarian indicators such as the dividend yield or the ratio of the price of the stock to the book value per share, an accounting measure of the value of a company's assets. Stocks with very high dividend yields or very low price to book value ratios also tend to earn abnormal returns after adjusting for risk.[2]

[1] De Bondt and Thaler (1989).

[2] It should be emphasised that, *ex ante*, returns are not guaranteed but involve some element of risk. The relationship between risk and return is fundamental to the theory of finance: in general investors will wish to maximise return for a

[*Cont'd. on p. 29*]

Although these findings are by no means conclusive (there is, for example, evidence that mean reversion in stock market indices was primarily a feature of the pre-Second World War period, and that its presence is very much weaker in more recent times), they do suggest that there may well be yet another market 'anomaly' to explain.

Long-Horizon Returns in the UK

Of perhaps more interest to us is whether such an anomaly is found for the UK. Some recent research has found that long-horizon returns (returns calculated over periods of from two to eight years) on price indices over the last 20 years or so are indeed predictable from past returns, but the pattern of auto-correlation is predominantly positive, so that high returns have a tendency to be followed by high returns.[1] This implies that stock prices exhibit *mean aversion*, so that market prices have a tendency to diverge from fundamental values over long periods.

Support for these findings of return predictability is provided by a complementary set of tests which examine whether stock prices are *too volatile* when compared with the variability predicted from a particular class of EMH model, that of the constant-discount present value model in which the current price of an asset is given by the present value of an appropriately discounted stream of expected future dividends to be paid on the asset. Although these tests have led to major debates about the econometric theory underlying them, *excess volatility** does appear to be a feature of the US stock market.[2] These findings provide support for return predictability because excess volatility can be shown to imply predictability of returns, and *vice versa*, so that the two approaches are, in fact, equivalent.[3] Similar evidence of excess volatility has been found for the UK.[4]

given level of risk or minimise risk for a given level of return. Hence both the risk and the return of an asset are important, which leads to returns being adjusted for their associated level of risk. Risk is often measured by the variability of returns.

[1] Mills (1991a).
[2] See the surveys by Shiller (1989, Chapter 4) and Gilles and LeRoy (1991).
[3] A formal demonstration of this is provided by Cochrane (1991).
[4] See Bulkley and Tonks (1989) and Mills (1992).

8. Other Financial Markets

WHAT ABOUT FINANCIAL MARKETS other than that for equities? Bond markets have been subjected to many of the excess volatility tests discussed above, the underlying efficient markets hypothesis being focussed on the term structure, stating that the current long interest rate is some weighted average of the current and expected future short rates. This implies that the excess return on holding a long rather than a short bond should be unpredictable. For the USA, there has been an (almost) consistent rejection of this *expectations hypothesis**, yet this has not led to its demise, particularly in policy discussions. Shiller *et al.* nicely compare this resistance of the theory to competing evidence with the famous Tom and Jerry cartoon plot:

> '[T]he villain, Tom the cat, may be buried under a ton of boulders, blasted through a brick wall (leaving a cat-shaped hole), or flattened by a steamroller. Yet seconds later he is up again plotting his evil deeds.'[1]

Most of the rejections were obtained when analysing US interest rate data from the 1960s to the early 1980s; however, when data before the setting up of the Federal Reserve in 1914 was analysed, the expectations hypothesis was supported.

In an examination of UK interest rate data from 1870 to 1988, the expectations hypothesis was rejected for pre-1914 data. Although the result is different from that for the USA, it is consistent with historical accounts of the period in which the dominant short-term financial instrument was the commercial bill, whose drawers were insensitive to changes in either expected or real interest rates and who could not move freely from one market to another. The hypothesis was also rejected for the inter-war years, which is again a confirmation of the conclusions reached from detailed historical research.[2]

The results for the post-1952 era are markedly different. Rejections of the hypothesis are confined to perpetuities (War Loan): this is understandable, for such stocks are rarely traded

---

[1] Shiller *et al.* (1983, p. 175).

[2] See Nishimura (1971) for an historical account of the pre-1914 period, and Howson (1975) for an inter-war account.

and their yield is determined from quoted prices rather than from prices determined in an active market. The return on these stocks was found to be predictable by past observations on the spread between their rate and the short interest rate and on the change in the short rate itself. There was little support for the rejection of the hypothesis for gilts using the data from the 1980s, although the evidence was somewhat stronger for observations prior to 1979. This may be a reflection of the stronger segmentation of the gilt-edged market in this period than in the later years from 1981 when the Bank of England refrained from making issues of stock at the long end of the market in an attempt to reduce yields that were perceived to be too high in relation to official interest rate expectations. Thus 'like Tom, the expectations hypothesis continues to fight another day!'.[1]

Perhaps the next most important market is that of the foreign exchanges, which is used by the media as a prime example of what they regard as an extremely volatile market, subject to fashions and fads. Hence the phrase 'runs on the pound' and extreme reactions to 'news announcements'.

Research on the London Foreign Exchange Market

Two interesting research projects have recently been carried out on the London foreign exchange market. Charles Goodhart has undertaken, with various co-researchers, an analysis of the continuous record of dollar-sterling rates quoted on the Reuters FXFX screen for a three-month period in 1989.[2] This very high frequency data set consists of more than 135,000 observations and can therefore be analysed in many different ways. Of particular interest are the results obtained from estimating models in which news effects are allowed to influence both the current level of the exchange rate and its conditional variance, that is, the current variance estimated using only past observations of exchange rates. In such models, the exchange rate is not a random walk, but is found to fluctuate around a constant mean, so that although news effects do have an influence, and

[1] Mills (1991b, p. 605).
[2] See, for example, Goodhart and Figliuoli (1991), and Goodhart *et al.* (1991).

alter both the level and variability of the series, these effects are only transitory and in time the rate returns to its equilibrium level.

The second project conducted a survey of the forecasts of some 20 chartists working in the foreign exchange market and compared their forecasts both with one another and with the forecasts obtained from statistical models, including a simple random walk.[1] It found substantial differences between individual chartists, with one chartist (known as M) appearing particularly accurate. Indeed, M was the only chartist to perform better than the random walk model in terms of forecast accuracy, all the others being markedly inferior. Moreover, more complex statistical models were less accurate than the random walk, and were even bettered by some of the chartists.

9. Are Markets Interlinked?

THE RESEARCH REPORTED so far has concentrated on violations of weak form efficiency. What about violations of the other two definitions of efficiency – for instance, semi-strong efficiency? In particular, is there evidence that financial markets are interlinked? There is *prima facie* evidence that national stock markets are so linked, because the different opening times of the markets round the world seem to enable shocks in one to spill over to the others as and when they open for trading: recall the movements in concert of the markets on what has since become known as Black Monday (19 October 1987). Statistical investigations by various researchers provide confirmation of this linking for stock, commodity price, and foreign exchange markets.[2]

For bond markets, it has been found that shocks are rapidly transmitted from one market to another, the effect being completed usually within two days.[3] The US and UK bond markets are evidently the most independent, the West German most open to international influences. Japan appears to act as a

---

[1] Allen and Taylor (1990).

[2] See, *inter alia*, Shiller (1989, Chapter 10), Kasa (1992), Baillie (1989), and Baillie and Bollerslev (1989).

[3] Mills and Mills (1991).

follower, reacting to unanticipated movements or 'innovations' in other markets, rather than its own innovations influencing others. Nevertheless, the speed of the reactions to outside innovations suggests that it would be difficult to earn unusual profits in a particular market by making trades based primarily on observed developments in the other markets.

Interactions between markets within the UK have also been investigated: for example, the relationship between the domestic money markets and the foreign exchange market.[1] It would seem that, whereas movements in the foreign exchange market have no influence on the money markets, the converse does not hold: developments in the inter-bank and gilt markets go on to influence the foreign exchanges.

Interactions Between Stock and Gilt Markets

A final example concerns interactions between the stock and gilt markets in the UK. Figure 5 presents graphs of the stock price index and associated dividend index, and the price index and a gilt yield index. Visual examination of the graphs suggests a strong positive relationship between prices and dividends, and a negative one between prices and gilt yields. These relationships can be formally established by using a recently developed econometric concept known as *cointegration** which leads to an equilibrium condition in which the ratio of the gilt yield to the dividend yield is a constant. There are also significant short-run interactions, most importantly that changes in gilt yields influence stock prices, rather than *vice versa*, but this equilibrium ratio is worthy of further attention. It is plotted in Figure 6, where it is given the name *confidence*. It was deemed to be one of the most important indicators of stock price movements by Arthur Ellinger, whose quote opened the discussion of such movements at the start of this paper and who coined the term, stating that

> 'technically it shows the changes in the investor's preference between fixed interest (i.e. gilts) and stock investments. More simply, it shows the state of the investor's liver'.[2]

The plot of confidence has two standard error (s.e.) bounds

---

[1] Mills (1991c).   [2] Ellinger (1971, p. 70).

Figure 5

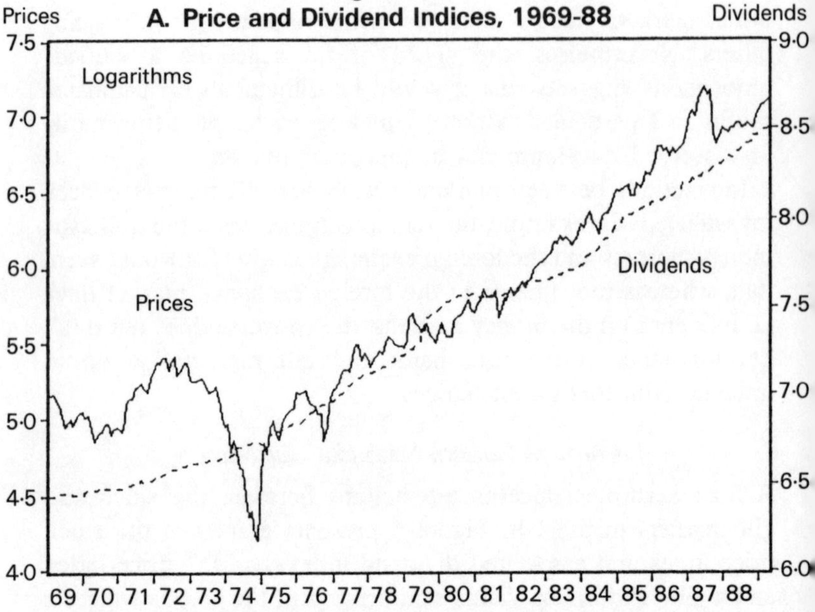

A. Price and Dividend Indices, 1969-88
Prices
Dividends
Logarithms
7·5
7·0
6·5
6·0
5·5
5·0
4·5
4·0
9·0
8·5
8·0
7·5
7·0
6·5
6·0
Prices
Dividends
69 70 71 72 73 74 75 76 77 78 79 80 81 82 83 84 85 86 87 88

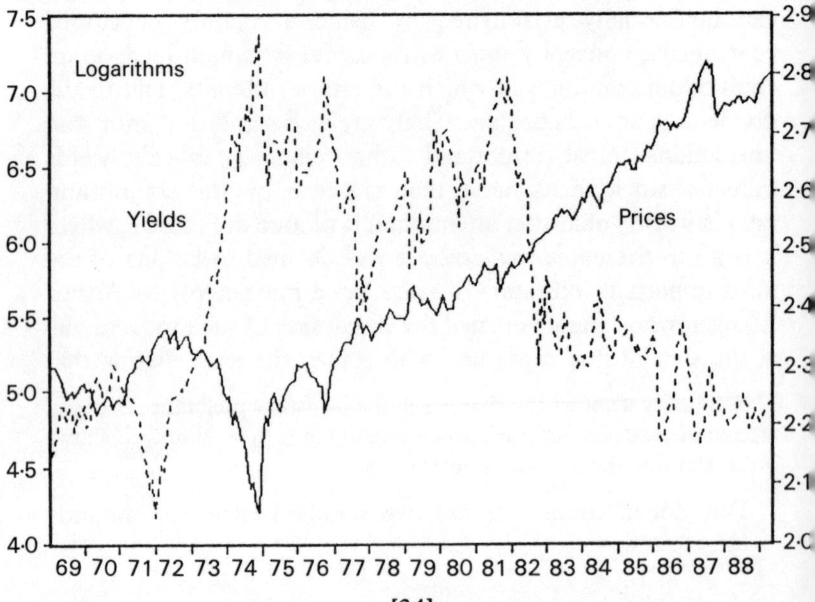

B. Stock Prices and Gilt Yields, 1969-88
Price Index
% p.a.
Logarithms
7·5
7·0
6·5
6·0
5·5
5·0
4·5
4·0
2·9
2·8
2·7
2·6
2·5
2·4
2·3
2·2
2·1
2·0
Yields
Prices
69 70 71 72 73 74 75 76 77 78 79 80 81 82 83 84 85 86 87 88

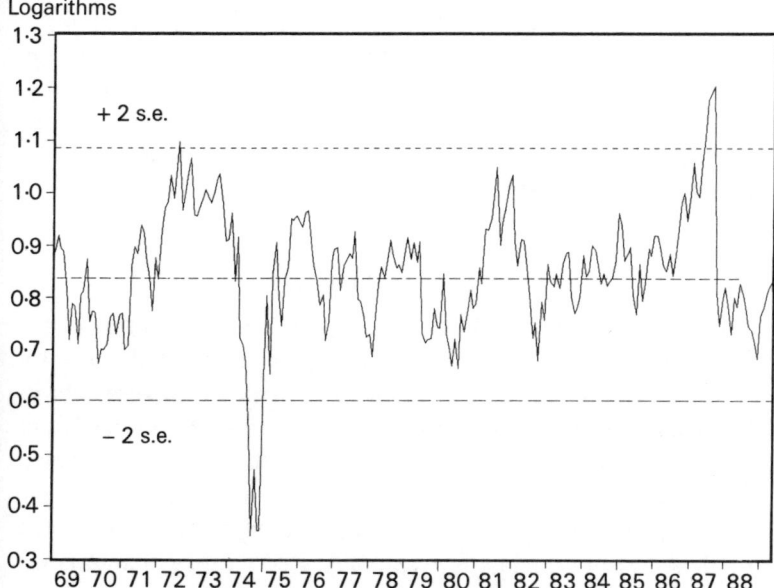

Figure 6
'Confidence', 1969-88

superimposed. While conventional probability statements should not be attached to these bounds, they do, nevertheless, seem to act as 'resistance lines'. Only during the latter months of 1974 and 1987 are they broken more than momentarily; at almost all other times a penetration is immediately reversed. Could the confidence factor be used as an indicator of future movements of the stock market? That would surely be an interesting line of research, given that many market commentators use this ratio, albeit informally, as an indicator of the relative performance of the two markets.

This research was presented in October 1990 at the autumn conference of the Institute for Quantitative Investment Research (known as INQUIRE) in Cambridge with a poignant outcome.[1] Although the econometric techniques underlying the results were inaccessible to the older investment analysts in the audience, there was great interest in resurrection of the 'Confidence Factor' as an equilibrium condition coming out of

[1] Since published as Mills (1991d).

such a 'fancy academic' model; most of these experienced analysts had been brought up on using the factor to monitor the stock and gilt markets in years gone by. One analyst recounted how Ellinger had trained him in the use of the factor in the 1950s and said how interested Ellinger would have been to have seen this demonstration of it in current action. Unfortunately, he added, Ellinger had died only the week before at his home in Cambridge.

10. Conclusions

To CONCLUDE, it may have seemed at the beginning of this paper that the aim was to show the absurdity of the methods used by chartists and technical analysts to predict future movements in financial markets and to trumpet the views of the academic Efficient Market Theorists. However, detailed investigations, using advanced econometric techniques, larger data sets, increasingly powerful computing ability, and alternative theoretical models, have in the last few years revealed a range of anomalies when the unpredictability-of-returns hypothesis is tested. Financial markets are often predictable to some extent, but the crucial question is whether this predictability can be exploited to make excess profits from trading in the markets. It is probably very difficult to do so, but that is unlikely to deter analysts and researchers from continuing to try to detect anomalies in the hope of uncovering, if only for a short while, a trading strategy that will 'beat the market'.

Glossary

In these explanations, an asterisk denotes that a term appears elsewhere in the Glossary.

Autoregressive Conditional Heteroskedastic (ARCH) Models

This is a class of models which, as well as having the current price change of an asset being a linear combination of past price changes (see linear and non-linear models), allows the current squared forecast error of the model to be a function of past squared forecast errors. It is an important model for analysing financial series because it provides a means of analysing a very noticeable feature of financial markets: the tendency for markets to go through protracted periods of calm interspersed with bouts of turbulence.

Chaotic Dynamics

Chaotically dynamic models, also known as models of deterministic chaos, have revolutionised the natural sciences in the last decade. They are models whose behaviour is perfectly predictable but which generate observations that look completely random under standard statistical tests. Since the price changes of many financial assets appear almost completely random (i.e. *independent**), the possibility of such changes being generated by deterministic chaos is obviously attractive. Research so far suggests, unfortunately, that such models for financial data are highly unlikely!

Chartism, Technical Analysis

These are terms for a set of techniques for predicting financial prices often based on observing patterns in price series that are supposed to recur regularly and hence have some prophetic significance. Other methods use a comparison of moving averages of different lengths.

Cointegration

Cointegration is a concept that has had a major influence in econometrics in recent years. Informally, two or more series are said to be cointegrated if, although each series individually has an upward trend to it, there is some (linear) combination of the series that is trend-free. This combination defines the long-run, or equilibrium, relationship between the series: they are thus 'bound together' over time. If there is no combination that is trend-free, then the series are not cointegrated, they are not bound together, and the concept of long-run equilibrium has little meaning.

Efficient Markets Hypothesis: Weak, Semi-Strong, Strong

A financial market is said to be *efficient* if it fully and correctly reflects all relevant information in determining asset prices. Formally, the market is said to be efficient with respect to some set of information if revealing that information to all participants would have no effect on prices. It is customary to distinguish three levels of market efficiency by considering three different types of information set.

The *weak* form of the *Efficient Markets Hypothesis* (EMH) asserts that prices fully reflect the information contained in the historical sequence of prices. Thus, investors cannot devise an investment strategy to yield better than average (abnormal) profits on the basis of past price patterns, i.e. by *chartism**. Changes in prices can therefore only occur because of unpredictable 'news' becoming available: price changes will therefore be unpredictable, the sequence of such changes will be *independent** of each other, or at least *uncorrelated**, and the price series itself will follow a *random walk**.

The *semi-strong* form of the EMH asserts that current stock prices reflect not only historical price information but also all publicly available information relevant to a company's shares. If markets are efficient in this sense, then an analysis of balance sheets, income statements, announcements of dividend changes or stock splits, or indeed any other public information about a company, will not yield abnormal profits.

The *strong* form of the EMH asserts that all information that is known to any market participant about a company is fully reflected in market prices. Hence not even those with privileged information can make use of it to yield abnormal profits: there is perfect revelation of all private information in market prices.

Expectations Hypothesis

The expectations hypothesis is one of the most popular theories for explaining the term structure of interest rates: the term structure concerns the relationship among yields of default-free assets that differ only with respect to their term to maturity, more popularly known as the shape of the yield curve. Informally, the theory states that the shape of the yield curve can be explained by investors' expectations about future interest rates: more precisely, long rates will be a weighted average of current and future short rates.

Excess Volatility

An alternative formulation of the *efficient markets hypothesis** is that the current price of a stock is the discounted sum of expected future dividends, in which case prices should not vary over time as much as the discounted sum of actual dividends, because a moving average is smoother than its components. The finding that prices vary more than this sum is known as excess volatility: it implies that prices are predictable and hence provides a violation of the efficient markets hypothesis.

Linear and Non-Linear Models

A linear model is one in which a variable, say the current change in the price of a financial asset, is related to a linear combination of other variables, say the past price changes of the asset. A non-linear model, on the other hand, relaxes the requirement that current price changes be a linear combination of past price changes, almost any type of combination being permissible.

Martingale

A martingale is related to, but is rather more general than, a *random walk**. It is the mathematical model of a *fair game*, one in which the expected price change (or return) is constant. The term 'martingale', which also denotes part of a horse's harness or a ship's rigging, refers in addition to a gambling system, originally popular in the French village of Martigues, in which the stake is doubled after each losing bet.

Mean Reversion and Long-Horizon Returns

Mean reversion refers to the possibility that asset returns measured over long periods of time (long-horizon returns, say, up to 10 years) are more predictable than short-horizon returns (those measured over, say, one month). This predictability will take a particular form: over long periods of time, prices will have a tendency to revert back to a 'trend line', determined by market fundamentals.

Random Variable

If the value of a numerical event varies in repeated sampling by chance, then it is called a random variable. Thus a sequence of price observations may be considered to be a sequence of random variables because the value taken by each observation will vary and may be thought of as occurring by chance, the probability of occurrence being then given by some assumed model.

Random Walk

A random walk is a time-series in which successive changes are *uncorrelated**. More precisely, a *strict* random walk is a time-series in which successive *changes* are *independent**. Often the average value of the changes is zero: when it is not, the random walk is said to have a *drift*.

Statistical Independence and Correlation

Two observations on a time-series are said to be independent if the value taken by one observation has no influence on the value taken by the other. It is important to note that no restrictions are placed on how the two observations could be related. If, however, we restrict attention to *linear* relationships, lack of independence implies that the two observations are *correlated*, which is thus a measure of *linear association*. Consequently, in the more general case, two observations may have no linear association, i.e. be uncorrelated, but still have some *non-linear* relationship existing between them: for example, their squares might be related. In this case the observations are uncorrelated but *not* independent.

Technical Analysis – see Chartism

Bibliography

Allen, H., and M. P. Taylor (1990): 'Charts, Noise and Fundamentals in the London Foreign Exchange Market', *Economic Journal*, Vol. 100 (Conference 1990), pp. 49-59.

Baillie, R. T. (1989): 'Commodity Prices and Aggregate Inflation: Would a Commodity Price Rule be Worthwhile?', *Carnegie-Rochester Conference Series on Public Policy*, Vol. 31, pp. 185-240.

Baillie, R. T., and T. Bollerslev (1989): 'Common Stochastic Trends in a System of Exchange Rates', *Journal of Finance*, Vol. 64, pp. 167-81.

Bulkley, G., and I. Tonks (1989): 'Are UK Stock Prices Excessively Volatile? Trading Rules and Variance Bounds Tests', *Economic Journal*, Vol. 99, pp. 1,083-1,098.

Cochrane, J. H. (1991): 'Volatility Tests and Efficient Markets', *Journal of Monetary Economics*, Vol. 27, pp. 463-85.

Cootner, P. A. (1964): (ed.), *The Random Character of Stock Market Prices*, Cambridge, Mass.: MIT Press.

De Bondt, W. F. M., and R. H. Thaler (1989): 'A Mean-Reverting Walk Down Wall Street', *Journal of Economic Perspectives*, Vol. 3(1), pp. 189-202.

Ellinger, A. G. (1971): *The Art of Investment*, London: Bowes & Bowes, 3rd Edition.

Fama, E. F. (1965): 'The Behaviour of Stock Market Prices', *Journal of Business*, Vol. 38, pp. 34-105.

Fama, E. F., and K. R. French (1988): 'Dividend Yields and Expected Stock Returns', *Journal of Financial Economics*, Vol. 22, pp. 3-25.

Feller, W. (1959): *An Introduction to Probability Theory and its Applications*, Vol. 1, 2nd Edition, New York: Wiley.

Gilles, C., and S. F. LeRoy (1991): 'Econometric Aspects of the Variance-Bounds Tests: A Survey', *Review of Financial Studies*, Vol. 4, pp. 753-91.

Goodhart, C. A. E., and L. Figiuoli (1991): 'Every Minute Counts in Financial Markets', *Journal of International Money and Finance*, forthcoming.

Goodhart, C. A. E., S. G. Hall, S. G. B. Henry, and B. Peseran (1991): 'News Effects in a High Frequency Model of the Sterling Dollar Exchange Rate', *Bank of England Discussion Paper, Technical Series*, No. 41.

Granger, C. W. J., and O. Morgenstern (1970): *Predictability of Stock Market Prices*, Heath: Lexington.

Howson, S. (1975): *Domestic Monetary Management in Britain 1919-38*, Cambridge: Cambridge University Press.

Hsieh, D. A. (1991): 'Chaos and Nonlinear Dynamics: Application to Financial Markets', *Journal of Finance*, Vol. 46, pp. 1,839-1,877.

Kasa, K. (1992): 'Common Stochastic Trends in International Stock Markets', *Journal of Monetary Economics*, Vol. 29, pp. 95-124.

Kendall, M. G. (1953): 'The Analysis of Economic Time-Series – Part 1: Prices', *Journal of the Royal Statistical Society*, Series A, Vol. 96, pp. 11-25.

LeRoy, S. F. (1989): 'Efficient Capital Markets and Martingales', *Journal of Economic Literature*, Vol. 27, pp. 1,583-1,621.

Mandelbrot, B. B. (1966): 'Forecasts of Future Prices, Unbiased Markets and "Martingale" Models', *Journal of Business*, Vol. 39, Supplement, pp. 242-55.

Mandelbrot, B. B. (1989): 'Louis Bachelier', in J. Eatwell, M. Milgate and P. Newman (eds.), *The New Palgrave: Finance*, pp. 86-88, London: Macmillan.

Mills, T. C. (1991a): 'Assessing the Predictability of UK Stock Market Returns Using Statistics Based on Multiperiod Returns', *Applied Financial Economics*, Vol. 1, pp. 241-45.

Mills, T. C. (1991b): 'The Term Structure of UK Interest Rates: Tests of the Expectations Hypothesis', *Applied Economics*, Vol. 23, pp. 599-606.

Mills, T. C. (1991c): 'Modelling Weekly Data on UK Interest and Exchange Rates', *Applied Economics*, Vol. 23, pp. 95-100.

Mills, T. C. (1991d): 'Equity Prices, Dividends and Gilt Yields in the UK: Cointegration, Error Correction and "Confidence"', *Scottish Journal of Political Economy*, Vol. 38, pp. 242-55.

Mills, T. C. (1992): 'Testing the Present Value Model of Equity Prices for the U.K. Stock Market', *Journal of Business Finance and Accounting*, Vol. 20, forthcoming.

Mills, T. C., and A. G. Mills (1991): 'The International Transmission of Bond Market Movements', *Bulletin of Economic Research*, Vol. 43, pp. 273-81.

Neftci, S. N. (1991): 'Naive Trading Rules in Financial Markets and Weiner-Kolmogorov Prediction Theory: A Study of "Technical Analysis"', *Journal of Business*, Vol. 64, pp. 549-71.

Nishimura, S. (1971): *The Decline of Inland Bills of Exchange in the London Money Market 1855-1913*, Cambridge: Cambridge University Press.

Pearson, K., and Lord Rayleigh (1905): 'The Problem of the Random Walk', *Nature*, Vol. 72, pp. 294, 318, 342.

Plummer, T. (1989): *Forecasting Financial Markets: The Truth Behind Technical Analysis*, London: Kogan Page.

Ramsey, J. B. (1990): 'Economic and Financial Data as Nonlinear Processes', in G. P. Dwyer and R. W. Hafer (eds.), *The Stock Market: Bubbles, Volatility, and Chaos*, Boston, Mass.: Kluwer Academic, pp. 81-134.

Roberts, H. V. (1959): 'Stock-Market "Patterns" and Financial Analysis: Methodological Suggestions', *Journal of Finance*, Vol. 14, pp. 1-10.

Samuelson, P. A. (1965): 'A Proof That Properly Anticipated Prices Fluctuate Randomly', *Industrial Management Review*, Vol. 6, pp. 41-49.

Shiller, R. J. (1989): *Market Volatility*, Cambridge, Mass.: MIT Press.

Shiller, R. J., J. Y. Campbell, and K. L. Schoenholtz (1983): 'Forward Rates and Future Policy: Interpreting the Term Structure of Interest Rates', *Brookings Papers on Economic Activity*, Vol. 1 (1983), pp. 173-217.

Stewart, T. H. (1986): *How Charts Can Make You Money: Technical Analysis for Investors*, Cambridge: Woodhead-Faulkner.

Thaler, R. (1987a): 'Seasonal Movements in Security Prices I: the January Effect', *Journal of Economic Perspectives*, Vol. 1(1), pp. 197-201.

Thaler, R. (1987b): 'Seasonal Movements in Security Prices II: Weekend, Holiday, Turn of the Month, and Intraday Effects', *Journal of Economic Perspectives*, Vol. 1(2), pp. 169-77.

Working, H. (1934): 'A Random-Difference Series for Use in the Analysis of Time Series', *Journal of the American Statistical Association*, Vol. 29, pp. 11-34.

Have the Banks Failed British Industry?
FORREST CAPIE and MICHAEL COLLINS

The question posed in the title of this *Hobart Paper* has been asked by critics of 'the City' many times over the years—but never answered satisfactorily. The authors here attempt an historical survey over a period of 120 years, from just before the decline of British industry began, divided into three periods.

In the period up to the First World War there was little demand from industry—then mainly family businesses—for support from the banks because of concern to retain family control. Most investment was financed by retained profits. In the period between the World Wars, when the joint-stock company was growing in importance, the banks appeared to continue their resistance to anything but short-term loans. No serious involvement with industry seems to have occurred until the Depression, when the decline in export markets led to large-scale unemployment, triggering growing demands for political intervention. This led to the Bank of England becoming involved in rescuing a key industrial client and in attempts at industrial reconstruction; the banks followed its lead in helping to set up new institutions to aid declining industries.

A continuing concern to plug the so-called Macmillan 'gap' after the Second World War led to a proliferation of institutions offering longer-term loans to smaller firms, but the banks also found themselves having to give increasing support to the expanding public sector. Throughout most of the period surveyed, British banks have shown a remarkable stability in contrast to their Continental and US counterparts, which suffered numerous destabilising liquidity crises. This stability, the authors say, may have been the best way of encouraging economic growth. The allegations that the banks (and 'the City') have been guilty of short-termism to the detriment of British industry and the economy generally are unproven, conclude the authors. The problem, if anything, lies on the demand, not the supply, side.

ISBN 0-255 36308-7   Hobart Paper 119

The Institute of Economic Affairs
2 Lord North Street, Westminster
London SW1P 3LB
Telephone: 071-799 3745

£6.95

For: Academic and business economists   Directors and managers
      Banks   Tax advisers and managers
      Financial service businesses   Government departments
      Policy makers   Interest groups

The State of the Economy 1993

IEA 4th Annual Conference

☆☆☆☆

*A special one-day conference bringing together
British and international economists
to assess the United Kingdom economy*

☆☆☆☆

With expert analysis of

★ **Monetary policy**
★ **Strategy for recovery**
★ **Future monetary arrangements in Europe**
★ **The property market**
★ **Government economic policy**
★ **Interest rates**
★ **German unification**
★ **Implications of the French referendum**
★ **Economic forecasting techniques**

and a keynote luncheon speech

☆☆☆☆

Thursday, 21 January 1993

**St. Ermins Hotel
Caxton Street
Westminster, London SW1**

☆☆☆☆

The Institute of Economic Affairs
2 Lord North Street
Westminster
London SW1P 3LB